LEGENDARY LEAGUES

LEGENDARY LEAGUES

MICHAEL COLEMAN

www.michael-coleman.com

Illustrated by
Mike Phillips

Hippo

Scholastic Children's Books,
Euston House, 24 Eversholt Street,
London NW1 1DB, UK
A division of Scholastic Ltd
London ~ New York ~ Toronto ~ Sydney ~ Auckland
Mexico City ~ New Delhi ~ Hong Kong

Published in the UK by Scholastic Ltd, 2001

10 digit ISBN 0 439 99910 3
13 digit ISBN 978 0439 99910 6

All rights reserved
Typeset by TW Typesetting, Midsomer Norton, Somerset
Printed and bound in Denmark by Nørhaven Paperback, Viborg

10 9

Contents

INTRODUCTION

Life is great when your team is at the top of the League. But when you're down at the other end, football can seem really foul…

The English Football League began in 1888 and is still going strong. Over the years the competition has seen triumphant teams and terrible teams, top teams and trembling teams. Teams like…

- The triumphant team who won the League title while playing on a beach.
- The terrible team who were belted 10-0 three times in one season.
- The top team whose manager wanted them to give their opponents a goal.
- The trembling team who only needed to score a penalty to become League champions.

THAT SINKING FEELING

In this book you'll discover foul facts you never knew about football league competitions throughout the world – but, most of all, you'll find out about the kind of crazy capers that have made the English Football League the most famously exciting league of them all. Like...

- The dribbling dog who saved a team from relegation.
- The crucial game which ended with nobody knowing what the score was.
- The time the League champions couldn't be awarded their trophy – because it had been "lost" by their deadly local rivals.

And, talking of trophies and awards, we'll be handing out our very own *Foul Football* awards to those who deserve them. Awards such as...

THE HOW NOT TO BE A GOOD ADVERTISEMENT FOR LEAGUE FOOTBALL ON THE TELLY AWARD...

Shared equally by **Blackpool** and **Bolton Wanderers**. Back in 1960, TV companies weren't sure viewers would be interested in watching live league games. As an experiment they showed a Friday-night First Division game between Blackpool and Bolton. Bolton won 1-0, but future TV viewers lost out badly. The match was so deadly boring that nobody had the courage to show another live league game until 1983 – 23 years later.

So, read on. This book is in a league of its own!

LEGENDARY LEAGUES TIMELINE

1872 The Football Association (FA) Cup competition begins. Clubs enter for this national competition and their own local knockout cup competitions. The rest of the time they play friendly matches against each other.

1886 A newspaper called *Football Field* uses scores from friendly games to try and work out which is the best team in Britain. Its decision: Preston North End. But are they right?

1888 The English Football League is formed. Just 12 clubs take part, all from the North and Midlands. And who are the first-ever League champions? Preston North End!

WHO SAYS YOU CAN'T BELIEVE WHAT YOU READ IN THE PAPERS!

PRESTON CHAMPIONS!

1890 A ten-club Scottish League begins.

1892 The Football League adds a Second Division. At the end of the season the bottom teams of the First Division play the top teams of the Second in "test matches" to decide who's going to be playing in which division the following year.

1892 The first inter-league match takes place between teams representing the Football League and the Scottish League. It was a 2-2 draw.

1893 (Woolwich) Arsenal go it alone and become the only southern club in the Football League. In 1894 the other main clubs in the South later set up their own league called – you've guessed it – the Southern League!

1898 Test matches are scrapped. The two most terrible teams in the First Division are now automatically relegated with the two top teams in the Second Division being promoted to take their place.

1915 The Football League closes down until 1919 because of the First World War. Only special wartime competitions are held.

1920 The 22 clubs in the top division of the Southern League all resign from their league to become the Third Division of the Football League. Arsenal are able to look down on them – because by now they're a First Division club!

1923 Another 22-team division is added! The Fourth Division? No. The new clubs are all from the North, so they make the Third Division (North) with the ex-Southern League lot becoming the Third Division (South).

1957 Footballers can now open their presents and stuff themselves with Christmas pudding. The tradition of playing League games on Christmas Day, with the return matches on Boxing Day is scrapped.

I KNOW IT'S CHRISTMAS, BUT YOU DON'T HAVE TO PLAY LIKE A TURKEY!

1958 Twenty-four teams are relegated from the Third division in one season! Apart from expanding to 24 teams each in 1950, the two Third Divisions haven't altered since 1923. That's the problem — only the two champions can win promotion every year. To liven things up, the bottom 12 teams of both divisions become the Fourth Division with four-up, four-down promotion and relegation.

1973 A three-up three-down promotion and relegation system is introduced between the old First and Second Divisions.

1979 Teams outside the Football League are generally known as non-league teams. A new league is formed from the best of them. It's called the Conference League. (Why? Who knows — maybe they were talking about the name for a long time!)

1987 Automatic relegation and promotion is introduced between the bottom team in the Football League and the top team in the Conference League. (In other words the league team becomes a non-league team and the non-league team becomes a league team!)

1987 League history repeats itself. Test matches are brought back to decide one of the three promoted teams in each division. The only difference is that they're called play-offs this time.

1988 The League is 100 years old and celebrates with a match between a Football League team and a Rest of the World Team. The Argentine star Diego Maradona is paid £90,000 to play for the World team.

WE'VE PAID £90,000, SO I DON'T WANT ANYONE TACKLING HIM, RIGHT?

1992 For the first time in its history the Football League gets smaller. All the top clubs join a new league called the Premiership (run by the Football Association). As a result the Football League shrinks by a whole division. To make the remaining clubs feel better, these divisions are renamed First, Second and Third. Apart from the name changes, hardly anybody notices.

The Football League in England was the first league competition in the world. So, who do we have to thank? Which bold, far-sighted Englishman had the idea in the first place?

Er – it wasn't an Englishman, actually. His name was William McGregor, and he came from Scotland...

THE FLYING SCOT:
WILLIAM McGREGOR

In 1888, William McGregor was 45 years old. He was a tubby, bearded man, the sort of Scotsman who looks as though he could toss a caber further than you or I could toss a pancake.

After living in Scotland all his life he'd decided to come to wealthier England. He'd bought a shop in Birmingham, selling cloth. It was just a couple of goal kicks away from Aston Villa's ground, Villa Park, so McGregor began to watch Villa's games. It wasn't long before he'd joined the group of men who ran the club ... and began having big ideas!

You are invited
to
McGregor's BIG
haggis party

R.S.V.P

His biggest idea came about because Aston Villa had a problem: money! Unlike the clubs in the South of England, whose players were mostly well-off and could afford to play the game for nothing, Aston Villa were a professional team. They paid their players wages.

Where did this money come from? From spectators handing over some of *their* wages to watch Villa's matches, of course. That was the problem. If loads of fans turned up they got loads of money, and loads of fans did turn up when Villa had big FA Cup matches. But once they were knocked out, all they had left until the following season were a few local Cup matches and lots of friendly games – which fewer and fewer fans were turning up to watch.

THE KIND OF MATCH MOST LIKELY TO MAKE A SPECTATOR STAY AT HOME AWARD...

A friendly match – because sometimes players stayed at home as well! When a team called Bootle met Everton in 1881, they turned up with only eight players and had to ask three spectators to play for them! (The fans must have been good – Bootle won the match 1-0!) Even worse, friendly games were often called off at the last minute. Without TV and radio bulletins, this meant that fans would turn up at an empty ground. Not surprisingly, they soon stopped turning up altogether!

WHERE'S OUR SUPPORT?

I BROUGHT MY MUM ALONG

William McGregor's big idea was to have a competition that would give top clubs like Aston Villa regular games every week (which meant regular money!). It was a league competition. He sat down and wrote a letter to the organizers of some other professional clubs...

I BEG TO TENDER THE FOLLOWING SUGGESTION... THAT TEN OR TWELVE OF THE MOST PROMINENT CLUBS IN ENGLAND COMBINE TO ARRANGE HOME-AND-AWAY FIXTURES EACH SEASON...

The other clubs were interested. On the Friday evening of 23 March, 1888 they had a meeting in a London hotel. William McGregor explained his big idea in more detail – with the result that everybody decided it wasn't only a big idea, it was a good idea!

Less than a month later, on 17 April, 1888, the formation of the Football League was announced!

I REALLY BELIEVE THAT THE GAME WOULD HAVE RECEIVED A SEVERE CHECK, AND ITS POPULARITY WOULD HAVE BEEN PARALYSED ONCE AND FOR ALL, IF THE LEAGUE HAD NOT BEEN FOUNDED.

The Football League was certainly William McGregor's biggest idea, but it wasn't the only one he had. The flying Scot was full of them! To find out some of the Big Ideas he was associated with, try this little Big Ideas quiz.

1 William McGregor liked the big idea of having his name on a new football boot. True or False?
2 William McGregor had the big idea of playing for Aston Villa himself. True or False?
3 William McGregor had the big idea of giving away the FA Cup after Aston Villa won it. True or False?
4 William McGregor liked the big idea of having his name on a new football. True or False?

5 William McGregor had the big idea of inventing a special hospital bed for injured footballers. True or False?

Answers:
1 True. During the 1890s you could buy the cheapest pair of McGregor football boots (as used by the players of Aston Villa – of course! – and lots of other teams) for 47p ... although if you wanted to be really flash you saved your pocket money and went for the top-of-the-range 68p model!

17

2 False. William McGregor didn't play football at all! He said: *I've never taken part in active football. I tried it once when I was very young and had to take to bed for a week.*

3 True – although he didn't do it on purpose. After Villa won the FA Cup in 1895, William McGregor loaned it to a boot and shoe shop (the same shop that made and sold McGregor football boots and footballs!) to display in their window. That night the Cup was stolen and never seen again.

4 True. You could get your kicks with a McGregor football if you could afford the price of 55p.

5 False – although an injured player could have found himself stretched out on a "McGregor Bed" in Birmingham Hospital. When the flying Scot died in 1911, the English and Scottish league clubs dedicated one of the hospital beds in his memory.

THE SCOTSMAN CLOSEST TO THE HEART OF EVERY FOOTBALLER WHO'S EVER APPEARED IN AN ASTON VILLA SHIRT AWARD...

William McGregor – whose big idea it was to have a raging lion put on the badge still found on every Villa shirt. Why? Because it reminded him of home – the Scotland team badge features exactly the same kind of lion!

LEAGUE LAWS

Twelve teams from the Midlands and the North of England joined William McGregor's first-ever Football League competition in 1888.

Question: Here are the names of 13 teams. Which is the odd one out in McGregor's competition?

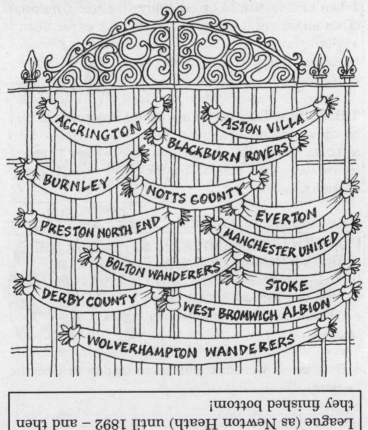

ACCRINGTON

ASTON VILLA

BLACKBURN ROVERS

BURNLEY

NOTTS COUNTY

EVERTON

PRESTON NORTH END

MANCHESTER UNITED

BOLTON WANDERERS

STOKE

DERBY COUNTY

WEST BROMWICH ALBION

WOLVERHAMPTON WANDERERS

But you can't just invent a competition and let the teams get on with it. You have to have rules. So before the League could get under way, William McGregor's League Management Committee had to work out what they were going to be...

How's your management? Could you have been a Committee Member? Find out in this decisive League laws quiz!

1 The League would be limited to 12 clubs, because of a shortage of – what?

a) Saturdays.

b) Teams that were good enough.

c) Referees.

2 How many League teams would any town or city be allowed to have?

a) One.

b) Two.

c) Any number.

3 How would a club qualify to join the League?

a) Beat an existing League team in the FA Cup.

b) Win an election.

c) Own a big enough ground.

4 How much would a club have to pay to join the League?

a) Nothing.

b) Less than £50.

c) More than £50.

5 How many League teams could a player play for during a season?

a) One.
b) No more than two.
c) Any number.

6 How many clubs would be relegated at the end of the League season?
a) None.
b) One.
c) Four.

OUT!

And, finally…
7 How many points would a team get for winning a League game?
a) Two.
b) Three.
c) Don't know.

THE MOST STUPID RULE AWARD…

The rule which said that abandoned games had to be continued from where they left off. On 26 November 1898, the match between Sheffield Wednesday and Aston Villa was abandoned because of bad light after 79-and-a-half minutes with Wednesday 3-1 ahead. Four months later, in March 1899, the two teams had to play the final 10-and-a-half minutes of the game!

Answers:

1a) The League wasn't seen as the most important competition to begin with. Clubs still wanted to enter the FA Cup and their local Cup competitions. Also, the football season only ran from September to April. This left only 22 free Saturdays for league games – and 22 home and away games meant a league of 12 clubs. (No, not 11 – teams don't play themselves, do they?!)

I CAN'T BELIEVE WE PLAYED OURSELVES AND LOST!

2a) Why? Probably because teams in the same town or city were already playing each other regularly in their local competitions. Playing different teams in the League would be less boring for the fans!

3b) A new club could only join the League if the other League clubs voted to let them in. So the Football League was a bit of a club, really.

4b) A lot less than £50, in fact. A mere £2.10p!

5a) A player could only turn out for one club during a season. No glory-hunting mid-season club-switches in those days!

6c) ... or b) ... or, more often, a) The rule was that the bottom four teams at the end of the season had to apply for re-election. That is, the other clubs had a vote on whether the worst teams should stay or be thrown out in favour of another club. This sometimes led to one team being thrown out, and sometimes none at all. After all – who wants to throw out a team they can beat!

7c) True! When the Football League kicked off on 8 September 1888, it still hadn't been decided how many points the teams were playing for...

What's the point?

And leave it they did – until another meeting on 21 November, 1888 ... over two months after League matches began!

Finally, though, the committee came to a decision. It would be two points for a win, and one point for a draw. It must have been a difficult decision, because that's how it stayed until three points for a win was introduced in 1981, 93 years later!

Average arguments

Having sorted out the points question, another decision had to be made. How were they to separate teams ending the season with the same number of points?

The choice came down to one of two methods...

I VOTE FOR GOALS SCORED. NICE AND SIMPLE

I VOTE FOR GOAL AVERAGE. TAKE THE NUMBER OF GOALS A TEAM SCORES AND DIVIDE IT BY THE NUMBER OF GOALS THEY LET IN. THIS GIVES A DECIMAL NUMBER WHICH CAN GO ON FOREVER. NICE AND COMPLICATED!

You may find it amazing, but the vote went for goal average! (Maybe they were better at maths in Queen Victoria's day.) This decision, like two points for a win and one for a draw, lasted a long time too – until 1976.

Brains warmed up? Calculators at the ready? Here are three averagely easy questions on goal averages...

1. NEWCRUNCHERS UNITED AND EVERLOSING FINISH ON THE SAME NUMBER OF POINTS. NEWCRUNCHERS SCORED 60 GOALS AND LET IN 30; EVERLOSING SCORED 90 AND LET IN 60.
WHO FINISHED HIGHEST?

2. LIGHTSWITCH TOWN AND TROTTINGALONG HOTSPUR FINISH ON THE SAME POINTS. LIGHTSWITCH SCORED 100 GOALS AND LET IN 100; TROTTINGALONG SCORED 40 AND LET IN 39.
WHO FINISHED HIGHEST?

3. BLANKBURN ROVERS AND CLOGENTRY PITY FINISH ON THE SAME NUMBER OF POINTS. BLANKBURN SCORE 20 GOALS AND LET IN 40; CLOGENTRY SCORE 10 GOALS AND LET IN 19.
WHO FINISHED HIGHEST?

Answers:

1 Newcrunchers' goal average is $60 = 30 \div$ exactly 2; Everlosing's goal average $90 = 60 \div 1\frac{1}{2}$ (1.5 in decimal-speak). So although Everlosing scored more goals Newcrunchers finished highest.

2 Lightswitch's goal average is $100 = 100 \div$ exactly 1; Trottingalong's goal average is $40 = 39 \div 1$ and a titchy bit (actually 1.025641 ... and on until you get bored). So Trottingalong finished highest.

3 Blankburn's goal average is $20 = 40 \div \frac{1}{2}$ (0.5 in decimals). Clogentry's goal average is $10 = 19 \div \frac{1}{2}$ and a titchy bit (actually 0.5263157 ... until you get bored again). So Clogentry finished highest.

Did it all really matter? Yes, as you'll see lots of times in this book, goal average was often vital. But the strangest goal average wrangle came at the end of the 1889–90 season...

- Bolton Wanderers finished on 19 points. So did Aston Villa.
- Whichever team finished lowest on goal average would have to apply for re-election, the other team were safe.
- Aston Villa had scored 43 goals and let in 51, for a goal average of 0.8431.
- As for Bolton, they'd scored 54 goals and let in 65 ... or 64!

That was the big problem. Amazingly, when Bolton had played their League game against Notts County, nobody had known what the final score was!

The referee had recorded the score as a 4-0 defeat for Bolton. In that case, Bolton's goal average was $54 \div 64 = 0.8307$, meaning they'd finished below Aston Villa in the re-election spot.

But Bolton protested, saying the score had been the one reported in the newspapers and they'd actually only lost 3-0, making their goal average $54 \div 65 = 0.84375$ – just a titchy bit better than Aston Villa's and condemning Villa to the re-election spot!

So, what did the League Management Committee do?

a) Take the referee's score and make Bolton apply for re-election.

b) Take Bolton's score and make Aston Villa apply for re-election.

c) Make both teams apply for re-election.

d) Make neither team apply for re-election.

Answer: d) They decided that as nobody really knew the true score of Bolton's game they would solve the problem a different way. How? By announcing that instead of the bottom four teams having to apply for re-election that year, only the bottom three would have to do it!

In 1976 the league organizers finally realized that goal average encouraged teams to go for a boring 1-0 win instead of an exciting 6-4 victory. So the goal average system was scrapped in favour of goal difference (goals scored minus goals let in). If two teams were level on points the one with the biggest goal difference would be put top. It made a lot of difference!

BAD NEWS. THEY'VE SCRAPPED GOAL AVERAGE

COUNTONIT CALCULATORS

Re-election ructions

Were terrible teams always re-elected to the League? In the first two League seasons, Stoke were a terrible team. How terrible? Terribly terrible!

● In 1888–89 they came bottom, with just 12 points from 22 games.
● In 1889–90 they came bottom again, this time with only 10 points.

At the end-of-season meeting, Stoke became the first club not to be re-elected. West Bromwich Albion joined the League in their place.

Question: What did Stoke do?
a) Apply for election again at the end of next season.
b) Wait until a second division was formed and apply for that.
c) Sulk and never join the League again.

Answer: a) After just one season out, Stoke were voted back in again – and they've been a League club ever since!

29

Disastrous Darwen were an even more terrible team. In 1891–92 they finished bottom of the new 14-team league, creating the rotten record of becoming the first team to let in more than 100 goals in a season (112). Like Stoke, Darwen weren't re-elected at the end of the season either.

Question: What did Darwen do?
a) Apply for election again at the end of next season.
b) Wait until a second division was formed and apply for that.
c) Sulk and never join the League again.

I'M NOT GOING BACK UNTIL THEY SAY SORRY!

Answer: a) and b) A second division was started the following season. Darwen applied for that and were elected – and so became the first team to be relegated!

Disastrous Darwen didn't last much longer as a League team, though. In 1898–99 they came bottom of an 18-team Second Division with just 9 points from 34 games. During the season they'd lost games 10-0 (three times!), 9-0 and 9-2. In fact, they'd broken their own rotten record and let in 141 goals this time!

Disastrous Darwen were dumped and haven't returned to the Football League since.

Re-election ructions continued well into the twentieth century – until 1987, in fact. Here's why:

- At the end of every season the bottom team in the bottom division, let's call them Useless United, would have to apply for re-election.
- Any other clubs who wanted to join the League would have to apply at the same time. There could be loads of them.

The League clubs would then have to vote on which team they liked best – Useless United, or any of the others...

This sneaky system only ended in 1987 when it was decided to scrap all voting. From then on, the bottom club automatically dropped out of the Football League, their place being taken by the champions of the Conference League.

Test match troubles

The creation of the Second Division in 1892–93 gave William McGregor and his Football League Committee another big idea: promotion and relegation. The terrible First Division teams would drop into the Second Division, and the terrific Second Division teams would take their place ... maybe.

Who went up and who went down was decided by "test matches" between the bottom three teams in the First Division and the top three teams in the Second Division, like this:

Bottom of First Division v Top of Second Division
Next-to-bottom in First Division v Runners-up in Second Division
Next-to-next-to-bottom in First Division v Third in Second Division
The test-match winning teams played in the First Division the following season, and the losers in the Second Division.

So, how well did it work? Use your judgment to decide what happened in the test matches at the end of that 1892–93 season. Based on their playing records, which teams do you think were promoted and which were relegated? Here are the teams and the test match fixtures:

First Division
Newton Heath, bottom with 18 points

v

Second Division
Small Heath, 1st with 36 points

Accrington, 15th with 23 points

v Sheffield United, 2nd with 35 points

Notts County, 14th with 24 points

v Darwen, 3rd with 30 points

Answers: Sheffield United and Darwen won their games so they were promoted – with Darwen setting another record and becoming the first-ever relegated team to be promoted! Accrington and Notts County were relegated. But ... Second Division champions Small Heath (later to change their name to Birmingham City) lost their game and stayed down, with terrible team Newton Heath staying up!

THE EVENTUALLY MOST SUCCESSFUL TERRIBLE TEAM AWARD...

Newton Heath – who, after this lucky escape and a few others later on, changed their name to ... Manchester United in 1902.

Clearly the test match system wasn't one of the best big ideas, so in 1895–96 the League Management Committee came up with a scheme to overcome the problem of deciding promotion and relegation on a single game. The two bottom First Division teams and the two top Second Division teams would play a mini-league competition with the top two teams being promoted to (or staying in!) the First Division.

This seemed a better idea ... until the test match mini-league of 1897–98, anyway. That year, Stoke and Burnley were two of the four teams. Here's a little of what happened during their match.

Neither Stoke nor Burnley were worried about winning the match. Why? Because this was their last game in the mini-league and they knew that a draw would leave them both in the top two promotion spots. So they agreed not to try and ended up playing the most boring match ever. There wasn't a single shot at goal!

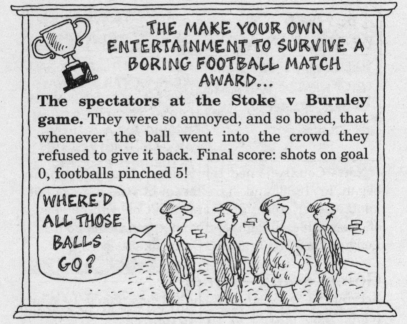

THE MAKE YOUR OWN ENTERTAINMENT TO SURVIVE A BORING FOOTBALL MATCH AWARD...

The spectators at the Stoke v Burnley game. They were so annoyed, and so bored, that whenever the ball went into the crowd they refused to give it back. Final score: shots on goal 0, footballs pinched 5!

WHERE'D ALL THOSE BALLS GO?

After this, test matches were scrapped and the top/bottom teams went up/down without any argument. Promotion and relegation had become "automatic".

GOODBYE! HELLO!

The oldest team in the Football League is Notts County. It was founded in 1862, but played very few matches against other teams in the early years. Why not? Because there weren't any other teams around, of course!

Notts County joined the Football League when it began in 1888 and have been in one division or another ever since. The same can't be said for loads of other clubs, though. Many have joined the Football League, then left it again. Clubs like these...

Going, going – gone!

Accrington were one of the 12 legendary League teams who played in the League when it began in 1888. They lost 2-1 to Everton on the first day, but managed to finish the season in the middle of the table. They resigned from the League in 1893 after losing their First Division

place to Sheffield United in a test match. Three years later, the club folded altogether.

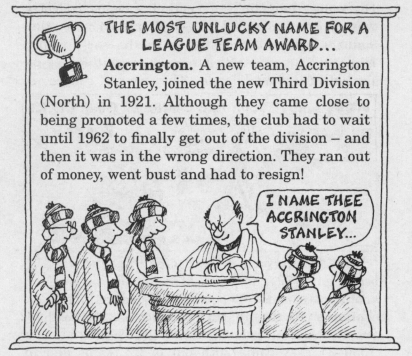

THE MOST UNLUCKY NAME FOR A LEAGUE TEAM AWARD...

Accrington. A new team, Accrington Stanley, joined the new Third Division (North) in 1921. Although they came close to being promoted a few times, the club had to wait until 1962 to finally get out of the division – and then it was in the wrong direction. They ran out of money, went bust and had to resign!

I NAME THEE ACCRINGTON STANLEY...

Glossop North End had a spectacularly "glossy" start to their league career. Joining the Second Division in 1898–99, they won promotion in their very first season. Then it all went wrong and life became more "loss" than "gloss". Winning only four out of their 34 games, Glossop went straight back down to the Second Division where they stayed until 1914–15 ... when they won only six out of 38 games and finished bottom! They didn't apply for re-election. **Nelson** – no, nothing to do with the famous Admiral, but a club which joined the Third Division

(North) when it began in 1921. A year later the flags were out as Nelson won promotion to the Second Division. After that, life got very choppy. Nelson were relegated in 1923–24, just missed promotion again the year after ... then began to sink horribly. In 1930–31 they lost 25 games in a row to end up on the bottom (of the League). They weren't re-elected.

LOOKS LIKE NELSON ARE CHANGING THEIR TACTICS

Thames flowed into the Third Division (South) for just two seasons before going down the plug-hole. In 1930–31 they came 20th out of 22 teams and in 1931–32 they finished bottom of the League and weren't re-elected. It couldn't have come as a surprise. Nobody loved Thames – not even their fans. In December 1930, only 469 turned up for their match against Luton, setting a record for the lowest attendance for a Saturday League game!

Wigan Borough set a record too, on 26th October 1931. Until then, clubs leaving the League had done so at the end of a season. Wigan didn't. They were the first League team to pack up in the middle of a season! So ... what happened next?

Answer: all Wigan's results were wiped out, as if the games had never been played. So teams who'd beaten Wigan ended up losing two points!

Perhaps the most sensational case of a club leaving the League was that of **Leeds City**. They'd joined the Second Division in 1905–06 and had never won promotion, almost always finishing in the middle of the table or lower. Then, at the end of the 1914–15 season, League football was scrapped because of the First World War.

In its place special war-time League competitions were held around the country. What's more, because many footballers had joined the army, navy or air force, they were allowed to turn out as guest players for the team nearest to where they were based to save them having to travel to their own clubs.

Suddenly, Leeds City began winning games! Between 1915–18, while the War was on, the team became amazing successful – so successful that they were actually declared League champions after winning play-off matches against the other war-time league winners.

What was the secret of Leeds City's success? Was it the fact that over 30 different players had turned out for them and seven of them were big international stars. Or was it...

a) Because Leeds had the only ground that hadn't been bombed.

b) Because they were all living in and around Leeds.

c) Because the club were breaking the rules and paying them too much.

Answer: almost certainly c). After the war ended in 1918, Football League officials asked Leeds City to show them the records of how they'd spent their money. The club refused, because they knew that if the records showed they'd done something wrong they could be thrown out of the League. So what did the Football League officials do to Leeds City? Threw them out of the League anyway!

Question: What happened to the Leeds City players?

a) They were auctioned.

LOT 50. AN EX-FOOTBALL PLAYER... WHAT AM I BID?

b) They were allowed to join any club they wanted.

c) They were banned from League football.

Answer: a) A big sale took place at a hotel and every Leeds City player was sold to the highest bidder! The cheapest went for £250 and the most expensive for £1,250 with the whole sale raising about £10,000.

Elland Road, the Leeds City ground, wasn't sold. The plan was for another club, Huddersfield Town, to move into it. But when Huddersfield decided against it, a completely new club was formed to take it over: it was called Leeds United – the famous club still playing there today.

Hello, Hello, Hello!
Clubs have joined the Football League in various ways. Match the clubs with their stories in this quiz.

Clubs
Arsenal, Chelsea, Liverpool, Manchester United, Peterborough United, Portsmouth, Scarborough, Wimbledon

Stories
1 They were elected to the Second Division of the League on 29 May 1905 – less than three months after the club had been formed! The first meeting of this club took place on 14 March 1905.

2 They were a Midland League club who'd beaten loads of Football League clubs in the FA Cup over the years. When they were finally elected to the Fourth Division in 1960 they won it at the first attempt!

3 They were the first club to rise from the Third Division to become League Champions.

4 After becoming the first non-league side to beat a top division team in the FA Cup three years previously, they were elected to the Football League in 1977–78. Just ten years later they were in the old First division and FA Cup winners!

5 They became, at the end of the 1986–87 season, the first team to be automatically promoted into the Football League from the Conference League.

6 They started off their League career in 1893 by impersonating a yo-yo. Joining the Second Division, they won promotion in their first season, were relegated in their second and promoted again in their third!

7 They were elected to the First Division in 1892, but started badly, finishing bottom two years running.

8 They were the first club from the South of England to be elected to the Football League, in 1893.

Answers:

1 – Chelsea. A man named Gus Mears owned a football ground (Stamford Bridge) – but didn't have a team!

THE PITCH LOOKS GOOD, THE STANDS ARE GREAT, THE CHANGING ROOMS ARE PERFECT. HOW'S THE TEAM COMING ALONG?

I KNEW I'D FORGOTTEN SOMETHING!

So he signed a lot of well-known players, telling them that they wouldn't have to stay if Chelsea didn't get elected to the League. Then he went to the League and told them he had a team of well-known players!

THIS IS MY TEAM, GENTLEMEN

FOOTBALL LEAGUE

AND HIM!

OOH, I KNOW HIM AND HIM!

AND HIM!

Chelsea were elected, finishing third in their first season and winning promotion the year after.

2 – Peterborough United who'd had to apply 21 times to get in, because the existing League clubs would always cast their votes for whichever one of their old pals had come bottom of the League

44

the year before. When Peterborough finally made it, in 1960–61, they became Fourth Division champions and their season's total of 134 goals is still a record!

3 – Portsmouth joined the new Third Division (South) in 1920 and gradually made their way into the old First Division to become champions in 1948–49.

4 – Wimbledon. The old First Division team they beat in the FA Cup in 1974–75 was Burnley. By 1987-88 they'd won promotion three times to reach the top division and were beating Liverpool 1-0 to win the FA Cup.

5 – Scarborough, who replaced Lincoln City.

6 – Liverpool. After these ups and downs, they stayed in the old First Division to win it for the first time in 1900–01.

7 – Manchester United (as Newton Heath). They've improved a bit since then!

8 – Arsenal ... 27 years before every other Southern club. Arsenal (then known as Woolwich Arsenal) joined the Second Division, reaching the old First Division ten years later in 1903–04.

LEGENDARY WORLD LEAGUES

Top teams

Only a top team can win the Football League Championship because only a top team is good enough to win matches throughout the sunny days of August, the wet days of November, the snowy days of January, the windy days of March until the season ends with some more sun in May.

THEY LOOK A BIT UNDER THE WEATHER!

LEAGUE CHAMPIONS

The first ever top team were Preston North End. They won the first League title in 1888. How top were they? So top that they didn't lose a single match all season!

That's a record that's never been equalled. But even Preston didn't manage to equal the legendary feats of these four top teams: Arsenal, Huddersfield Town, Liverpool and Manchester United. What did they do that was so special?

Answer: They all won three League championships in a row – Arsenal 1933–35, Huddersfield 1924–26, Liverpool 1982–84 and Manchester United 1999–2001. They're the only teams to have managed the feat so far, but lots of others have won the League title at different times. Some have never managed it, though!

Question: How many of these clubs have NOT won the League championship?

Aston Villa

Blackburn Rovers

Burnley

Chelsea

Ipswich Town

Derby County

Everton

Leeds United

Manchester City

Newcastle United

Nottingham Forest

Portsmouth

Sheffield United

Sheffield Wednesday

Sunderland

Tottenham Hotspur

Wolverhampton Wanderers

West Bromwich Albion

West Ham United

Answer: Only West Ham United. (Boo-hoo!) Aston Villa first won the title in 1893–94, Blackburn Rovers in 1911–12, Burnley in 1920–21, Chelsea in 1954–55, Derby County in 1971–72, Everton in 1890–91, Ipswich Town in 1961–62, Leeds United in 1968–69, Manchester City in 1936–37, Newcastle United in 1904–05, Nottingham Forest in 1977–78, Portsmouth in 1948–49, Sheffield United in 1897–98, Sheffield Wednesday in 1902–03, Sunderland in 1891–92, Tottenham Hotspur in 1950–51, West Bromwich Albion in 1919–20, Wolverhampton Wanderers in 1953–54. Who knows if West Ham will ever win it!

THE MOST LEGENDARY PIECE OF CHAMPIONSHIP-WINNING TIMING AWARD...

Shared between **Chelsea** and **Portsmouth.** They both won their first League titles exactly 50 years after being formed.

IT'S ABOUT TIME!

HALF PAST FOUR

The championships that Ipswich (1961–62) and Nottingham Forest (1977–78) won also had something legendary about them. Was it because:

a) They'd won the League with five games to go.

b) They'd only been promoted the season before.

c) They'd lost a game 0-8 during the season.

Legendary last-gasp winners

Sometimes one team is so far ahead the bid for the League title isn't very exciting at all. On other occasions it's such a close race that nobody knows who's going to win the League until the very last matches of the season.

Here's a quiz about last-minute title races. Can you work out what happened next?

1 It's the 1971–72 season. Derby County are top of the League, but they've finished their games. Leeds United only need to draw in a Monday night match against Wolverhampton Wanderers to take the title. What happens next?

a) Leeds win and become champions.

b) Leeds draw and become champions.

c) Leeds lose and Derby become champions.

2 It's the last match of the 1988–89 season. Liverpool don't even need to win their last match, at home against Arsenal. They can lose 0-1 and they'll still be champions. But if they lose 0-2 or worse, Arsenal will be champions! With just seconds to go, Arsenal are ahead 1-0. What happens next?
a) Arsenal score again and become champions.
b) Arsenal hit the bar and Liverpool become champions.

c) Liverpool equalize and become champions.

3 It's the last day of the 1923–24 season and Cardiff City are one point ahead of Huddersfield. In the final matches, Huddersfield win two points by beating Nottingham Forest 3-0; as for Cardiff, they're drawing 0-0 with Birmingham when ... they're awarded a penalty! What happens next?
a) Cardiff score the penalty, win the match and become champions.
b) Cardiff miss the penalty, draw the match, and Huddersfield become champions on goal average.
c) Cardiff miss the penalty, draw the match, but still become champions on goal average.

4 It's the last game of the 1970–71 season. Arsenal need to win or draw 0-0 to become champions. If they lose, or it's any other kind of draw, then the title will go to Leeds United on goal average. As if that isn't tricky enough, Arsenal's last game is against their deadly local rivals Tottenham Hotspur. What happens next?

a) Spurs win 1-0, so Leeds become champions.

b) Arsenal win 1-0 and they become champions.

c) Spurs miss a penalty, it's a 0-0 draw and Arsenal become champions.

5 Finally, one from the Second Division. Rotherham are playing Liverpool in a vital match at the end of the 1955–56 season. One of the two teams needs a huge win to guarantee promotion to the old First Division on goal average. What happens next?

a) Rotherham win 6-1 but still don't get promoted.

b) Liverpool win 6-1 and get promoted.

c) Liverpool win 6-1 but still don't get promoted.

Answers:

1c) Derby didn't bother to stay around to find out what happened. They went off to Majorca for a holiday. That's where they heard the good news!

2a) Michael Thomas of Arsenal scored with the last kick of the season! Later in his career he left Arsenal to join – Liverpool!

3b) None of the regular Cardiff penalty-takers fancied such an important kick, so an unhappy Len Davies stepped up to take his first-ever penalty ... and had it saved by the Birmingham goalkeeper! Cardiff and Huddersfield ended up with the same number of points but Cardiff's goal average $(61 = 34 \div 1.79)$ was just a titchy bit worse than Huddersfield's $(60 = 33 \div 1.81)$ and they had to settle for second place.

WE DON'T BLAME YOU, LEN. GO ON, YOU CAN GET IN THE BATH FIRST

4b) The goal was scored by Arsenal's Ray Kennedy – just two minutes from the end of the match!

5a) Yes, it was Rotherham who were the team after promotion – but even though they won 6-1 it wasn't good enough to give them a better goal average than the clubs ahead of them, Birmingham City and Luton Town. To go up they'd have needed to win 17-0!

Miserable fact for Rotherham fans #1: Nowadays, with three points for a win, Rotherham would have been champions and won promotion!

Miserable fact for Rotherham fans #2: Less than ten years later, the team they whacked, Liverpool, had become League champions. Rotherham never did get promoted; instead, they were relegated in 1967–68.

THE "NOW WHERE DID WE PUT THAT TROPHY, IT'S GOT TO BE AROUND HERE SOMEWHERE" AWARD...

Manchester United. United had won the League Championship in 1966–67. A year later their deadly rivals Manchester City took the title from them, winning the League before the end of the season – with United in second place. But when City asked to have the championship trophy presented at their last home game, United's officials "couldn't find it". Surprise, surprise, once City's game was over the trophy was discovered in the bank vault that United had used to stop nasty people getting their hands on it! City hurriedly arranged a special friendly match to let their fans see them receive it.

HOMES, AWAYS AND DRAWS

Strange as it may sound, football fans haven't always wanted to see their favourite team win. Sometimes they've been hoping and praying that they'd draw instead. Why? Because they'd picked them as one of their matches on their football pools coupons.

Newspaper football competitions started in the 1890s. An early favourite asked readers to predict the results of all the First Division matches on any Saturday. They had to say whether the match would be won by the home team, the away team or if it would be a draw.

Try an "easy" version of it for yourselves! Here are some of the matches played during the opening two weeks of the first-ever Football League season in 1887–88. Were they home wins, away wins or draws? To help you with the "form" of the teams, the numbers in brackets tell you the team's league position at the end of the season!

MATCH		HOME	AWAY	DRAW
(A) BLACKBURN ROVERS (4) V ACCRINGTON (7)				
(B) BOLTON WANDERERS (5) V DERBY COUNTY (10)				
(C) PRESTON NORTH END (1) V BURNLEY (9)				
(D) STOKE (12) V WEST BROMWICH ALBION (6)				
(E) WOLVERHAMPTON W (3) V ASTON VILLA (2)				

Results: A – draw, B – away, C – home, D – away, E – draw.

If you got those five right, then amazingly well done ... but you'd have had to forecast another four games correctly to win the prize; by the early 1900s there were nine matches every Saturday!

HOW DO I KNOW IF CITY ARE GOING TO WIN? I'M ONLY THEIR MANAGER!

By 1911, with the number of matches increasing to ten, getting them all correct was nearly impossible. So a Sunday newspaper, *The Umpire,* introduced an "easier" game with just six games. All you had to do was predict what the scores would be and you'd win £300.

Try it for yourselves, using the same five matches from 1887 as before. Now you know who the winners and losers were it should be a piece of cake! And to help you even more, the numbers after the team names tell you how many goals they scored in the whole of that opening season of 22 matches each.

MATCH	RESULT	SCORE
Ⓐ BLACKBURN ROVERS (66) V ACCRINGTON (48)	DRAW	
Ⓑ BOLTON WANDERERS (63) V DERBY COUNTY (41)	AWAY WIN	
Ⓒ PRESTON NORTH END (74) V BURNLEY (42)	HOME WIN	
Ⓓ STOKE (26) V WEST BROMWICH ALBION (40)	AWAY WIN	
Ⓔ WOLVERHAMPTON W (50) V ASTON VILLA (61)	DRAW	

Scores: A: 5-5, B: 3-6, C: 5-2, D: 0-2, E: 1-1

If you got those right you're either at least 110 years old and with a very good memory, incredibly lucky, or you looked at the answers first!

Correctly forecasting even a couple of scores was very hard and newspaper readers soon wanted a competition that looked a bit easier – even if it wasn't. So along came a different game altogether …

Spot the ball competitions were a lot harder than that one. The pictures used were always the sort which had players losing sight of the ball, so that to get it right you had to guess that the ball was balanced on the goalie's right ear or something like that. Maybe that's why the most regular winners were readers who didn't know anything about football at all!

Competitions to forecast the results of matches were still very popular, though. By the 1930s the best one was known as *football pools* – or "the pools" for short – because all the money sent in was "pooled" to give a huge prize to the winner ... or winners. Here's an idea of how it worked.

- Every week a coupon was printed showing all the English (and some Scottish) League matches being played that Saturday.

- You had to pick eight matches you thought would end in a draw. You wrote them down on the coupon and sent it in with your stake money. How much? About $\frac{1}{2}$ p! But most people staked a lot more by choosing loads of different eight-match groups.

- After the games were played, you worked out how many points your eight selections had earned you. A draw was worth three points, an away win two points and a home win a measly, useless one point.

- If you had the maximum 24 points, you'd got a "first dividend". You were a winner!

- You sent in your claim to the pools company, then waited anxiously to find out how much you'd won...

Question: Let's say enough stake money was sent in for the "pool" of prize money to be £1 million. How much would you win if you'd got the maximum 24 points for correctly forecasting eight draws?
a) £1 million.
b) £0·5 million.
c) £10.

Answer: a) ... or b) ... or, possibly, c)! It was like the National Lottery today. The prize pool was shared between the number of winners. If on any Saturday there were only eight drawn games and you were the only one to pick them – then all that lovely money was yours! But if it was a week with 20 drawn matches, the chances were that loads of people had picked eight of them – and the more winners there were, the less you got!

A FIRST DIVIDEND! GOOD JOB I'M NOT THE SORT OF IDIOT WHO FORGETS TO POST HIS POOLS COUPON!

POOLS COMPANY

The Pools Quiz

Try to forecast the eight correct answers in this pools quiz. You get three points for a correct answer and either two points or one point for a wrong answer (because some are a lot more wrong than others). Will you win a first dividend?

1 Only games played on a Saturday counted.	True ☐ False ☐
2 The pools companies have never paid the Football League for using their lists of League matches.	True ☐ False ☐
3 A postponed match was worth nothing.	True ☐ False ☐
4 During the 1970s League matches became so boring that the pools rules were changed to make only a score draw (1-1, 2-2 etc) worth three points.	True ☐ False ☐
5 In 1936 the Football League tried to stop the pools companies using their fixture lists by waiting until the middle of the week before telling clubs who they were playing on the Saturday.	True ☐ False ☐

6 By the 1990s pools coupons didn't even list the games being played.	True ☐ False ☐
7 In the terrible winter of 1963, so many matches were being postponed that the pools companies invented the results.	True ☐ False ☐
8 If only eight matches out of the 56 listed on a pools coupon were draws, the odds against you picking all eight would be nearly nine and a half million to one.	True ☐ False ☐

Answers:

1 – True (3 points). *If you said False – 1 point.* A listed game played on a Friday evening, for instance, only scored the same as a home win. It was to stop people cheating by filling in a Friday night draw and rushing to stick their coupon through the pools company's front door first thing Saturday morning!

OUT OF THE WAY! LAST MINUTE POOLS COUPON COMING THROUGH!

It didn't happen often, though. In those days, before TV companies decided kick-off times, virtually every game was played on a Saturday afternoon.

2 – False (3 points). *True – 2 points.* Although the pools companies were making a fortune every week, the Football League didn't get a bean until 1959.

3 – False (3 points). *True – 1 point.* It was actually worth the same as a home win – but as that meant you'd never win a first dividend, it amounted to next to nothing.

4 – True (3 points). *False – 2 points.* There may have been some entertaining 0-0 draws, but defensive play was producing so many draws every week that nobody was winning a big prize any more.

5 – True! (3 points). *False – 1 point.* But this meant that clubs couldn't tell their fans who they were playing either. All they could do was put a poster outside the ground saying something like UNITED vs ??? and fill in the missing name when they found out!

This mad scheme was scrapped after three weeks.

6 – True (3 points). *False – 1 point.* They thought it was off-putting for people who didn't know anything about football – and as the biggest prizes came when the drawn matches were all surprise results, knowing a lot about football probably didn't help anyway!

So every game was given a number and all you had to do was pick eight numbers (a bit like the lottery). If those games ended up as draws you were a winner.

7 – True (3 points). *False – 2 points.* A "Pools Panel" of ex-players (and even an ex-referee!) was set up to predict what the results of the postponed matches would have been.

8 – False (3 points). *True – 0 points – because you're a thousand times out!* The odds against picking 8 out of 56 are nearly nine and a half thousand million to one!

How did you get on?

24 points – you win a first dividend and scoop the pool!

23 or 22 points – you're good enough to win smaller prizes called second and third dividends

Less than 22 points – bad luck; try again next week!

UPS AND DOWNS

Teams who aren't in the top division of the League want to get there. Teams who are in the top division want to stay there!

Promotion and relegation is what spurs teams on – or scares them to death! Here are the ups and downs rules as they stand today:

FA PREMIERSHIP: Bottom three clubs relegated to the First Division.

FIRST DIVISION: Top two clubs promoted to the Premiership, plus the winner of "play-off" matches between the clubs who finished in third to sixth places. Bottom three clubs relegated to the Second Division.

SECOND DIVISION: Top two clubs promoted to First Division, plus the winner of "play-off" matches between the clubs who finished in third to sixth places. Bottom four clubs relegated to the Third Division.

MORE ➡

THIRD DIVISION: Top three clubs promoted to the Second Division, plus the winner of "play-off" matches between the clubs who finished in fourth to seventh places. The poor bottom club is thrown out of the Football League and their place taken by a club from the Conference League.

EXTRA LARGE FOOTBALL BOOTS FOR SALE! FOR THOSE BIG GAMES!

THE MOST MISERABLE CONFERENCE LEAGUE CHAMPIONS AWARD...

Stevenage Borough. After winning the Conference League in 1995–96, Stevenage weren't allowed to replace bottom club Torquay United in the Third Division – because their ground wasn't good enough!

Perilous play-offs

The rules nowadays mean that a team can still win promotion even if they don't finish higher than sixth in their league – almost exactly the same as when test matches were scrapped over 100 years ago!

Question: So how many of these three arguments were used for bringing back much the same scheme for the 1986–87 season?

a) To help make the old First Division smaller.

b) To provide end-of-season excitement for more teams.

c) To make more money from the extra matches.

Answer: all three, because:

a) The old First Division clubs were moaning about playing too many games, so it was decided to reduce it from 22 teams to 20 by using play-offs to throw out (or not promote) one team a year for two years. But because this affected the other divisions, play-offs had to be introduced for all of them.

b) Once they'd been started, clubs found they had more to play for. Even if they couldn't win their league, they might be able to get into a play-off position. This also kept fans' excitement up for much longer, meaning they'd be prepared to pay out to watch more matches. So, even after the old First Division had lost its two teams, play-offs stayed.

c) Although they said the extra money wasn't important, none of the clubs ever gave it back or let fans in for nothing!

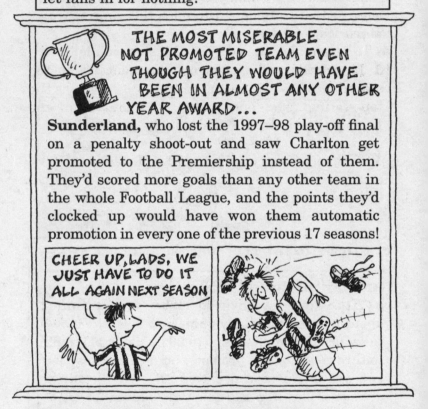

THE MOST MISERABLE NOT PROMOTED TEAM EVEN THOUGH THEY WOULD HAVE BEEN IN ALMOST ANY OTHER YEAR AWARD...

Sunderland, who lost the 1997–98 play-off final on a penalty shoot-out and saw Charlton get promoted to the Premiership instead of them. They'd scored more goals than any other team in the whole Football League, and the points they'd clocked up would have won them automatic promotion in every one of the previous 17 seasons!

CHEER UP, LADS, WE JUST HAVE TO DO IT ALL AGAIN NEXT SEASON

The promotion and relegation quiz
Can you spot a promotion prospect? How about picking out a team that's ready for relegation? Test your talents with this quiz!

1 It's the 1930–31 season and Manchester United have lost their first 12 games in the old First Division! Are they relegated, or do they survive?

2 At the end of the 1974–75 season Carlisle United, newly-promoted to the old First Division, are relegated again. Could you have predicted it? Where were Carlisle after just three First Division games? Top or bottom?

3 Manchester City, League champions and top scorers in 1936–37, finish the 1937–38 season as the top-scoring team once more. Do they retain the League title or are they relegated?

4 Stockport County set a record on 6 January, 1934: against Halifax Town in the Third Division (North) they became the first team to win a League game 13-0. Were they promoted, relegated – or neither?

THIRTEEN! UNLUCKY FOR SOME

YEAH, OUR GOALIE, WHEN I GET MY HANDS ON HIM!

5 At the end of the 1914–15 season, Tottenham Hotspur are bottom of the old First Division.

Because of the First World War, the League competition is abandoned until 1919–20. Are Spurs allowed to stay in the First Division because there's been so long a gap, or are they relegated?

6 It's the last day of the 1926–27 season and Portsmouth and Manchester City are neck-and-neck for promotion. They have the same points. Manchester City's goal record is 100-61, Portsmouth's 82-48. Manchester City win their last game 8-0 and Portsmouth win theirs 5-1. Which of them is promoted? (Calculators may be used!)

7 It's the 1935–36 season. Blackburn Rovers and Aston Villa are the only two of the original 12 league teams of 1887 never to have been relegated. Aston Villa need to beat Blackburn to stay up. Do they win and survive, or lose and get relegated?

8 It's 23 March, 1974 and Middlesbrough are playing Oxford United in the old Second Division when Middlesbrough manager Jack Charlton suddenly starts running up and down the touchline shouting at his players, "Give 'em a goal!" When the match ends, one of the teams has won promotion. Middlesbrough or Oxford?

9 On 1 September, 1979, Bristol City were in sixth place in the old First Division. Where were they by 4 December, 1982 – in the old Third Division or Fourth Division?

Answers:
1 They're **relegated** by a mile and their losing start is still a record.
2 Carlisle were **top**, with three wins out of three and no goals conceded!
3 Amazingly, they finished second-last and became the first reigning League champions to be **relegated**!

Even though they scored more goals (80 in 42 games) than any other team, they let in 77. The only team to let in more than that were West Bromwich Albion – and they came bottom.
4 Neither. Although their record win had helped them score 115 goals in 42 games, Stockport could only finish in third place.
5 Spurs were still **relegated**, even though an extra two teams were added to the Division. Worse, a vote which decided whether they should

stay, or be replaced by one of the high-finishing Second Division clubs from 1914–15, was won by their deadly rivals Arsenal – even though Arsenal had only finished in fifth place. Spurs got their own back, though. They won the 1919–20 Second Division championship in style.

6 Portsmouth whose goal average of 1.776 was just better than miserable Manchester City's 1.771!

7 They lost 4-2, finished second-last and were **relegated**. Blackburn weren't happy, though. In spite of the win, they finished bottom and were relegated as well!

8 Middlesbrough. They were way ahead of every other team in the Division and only needed one more win to clinch promotion. Jack Charlton wanted to do this in front of the Middlesbrough fans, not away at Oxford. So when his team went 1-0 up he pleaded with them to let Oxford draw level. They didn't.

9 In the **Fourth Division** – and on the bottom! They'd dropped 86 league places in just 3 years 95 days!

Great escapes

The season is drawing to a close. Useless United are rooted at the bottom of the League. Is there any way they can escape the big drop? Yes, there is. All they've got to do is win all their last four games by at least 15-0...

I KNOW IT SEEMS HOPELESS, BUT I THINK WE CAN PULL IT OFF

The history of the Football League is sprinkled with cases of teams who have managed to come good at the last minute and escape relegation when everybody – often including their own fans – thought they were doomed. Cases like these...

Lively Lincoln

With six games left of the 1957–58 season, Lincoln City were at the bottom of the old Second Division. To stand any chance of staying up, they had to win all six games – an unlikely feat, considering they'd only won five of their 36 games so far! But they won the first ... then the second ... and the third, the fourth ... and the fifth!

The sixth game was at home to Cardiff City. At half-time the score was 0-0. Then, just after the restart, Cardiff scored! Back came Lincoln to equalize. Then they went ahead! Finally, they scored again to run out winners 3-1. They'd escaped relegation by a single point.

Torquay's "dogged" display

It was the last day of the 1986–87 season. Torquay United needed to get a draw in their match against Crewe Alexandra. If they didn't they'd finish last in the old Fourth Division and become the first team to be automatically thrown out of the Football League.

But with just eight minutes to go, Torquay were 1-2 down.

It got worse. Torquay's defender, Jim McNichol, sank to the ground injured.

Then it got even worse – especially for McNichol. An over-excited police dog named Ginger ran on to the pitch and sank his teeth into McNichol's leg! Talk about a biting tackle!

That wasn't the end of the tail, though! As the 90 minutes drew to a close, Torquay were still losing. But the referee didn't blow for full-time.

He'd added on the five minutes of injury time it had taken defender McNichol to recover from Ginger's jaws. On the game went – until, in the very last minute, Torquay raced through to make it 2-2 and win the point they needed to stay up. They'd survived the relegation dog-fight!

Frantic Forest

Back in 1908–09, the situation at the bottom of the old First Division was very tight. Leicester Fosse were already relegated, but with two games to go any one of six teams could join them. Nottingham Forest were one of those teams; what's more, their goal average was just about the worst of the lot.

So when Forest ran out to play lowly Leicester, what they frantically needed wasn't just a win but a really good win. Ninety minutes later, they'd got it. Leicester had been given a terrific 12-0 trouncing and Forest's goal average was glowing!

The League was suspicious. Had something sinister been happening in the Forest? They held an inquiry – and discovered … what?

a) The Leicester players had happily lost the match because they'd been bribed.

b) The Leicester players had happily lost the match because they knew it would mean Manchester City being relegated with them.

c) The Leicester players had happily lost the match because they'd been happy, not because they'd lost.

Answer: c) The inquiry discovered that the whole Leicester team had been to a wedding the day before the game and were still seriously sozzled at kick-off time! The result was allowed to stand, Nottingham Forest escaped relegation and Manchester City went down instead.

Wonderful Walsall and shattered Sheffield

It was 2 May, the last day of the 1980–81 season, and in the old Third Division Walsall were playing Sheffield United. As the game moved into its final minute, Sheffield United were awarded a penalty.

Up stepped Don Givens ... and missed.

Sheffield United had lost 0-1 and were relegated. If the penalty had gone in, and the game ended as a 1-1 draw, Sheffield would have stayed up. And who would have gone down instead? Walsall!

Crazy Carlisle

But perhaps the most amazing escape from relegation ever took place on the final day of the 1998–99 season. Again it happened down at the foot of the Third Division, where Carlisle United were facing the big drop out of the Football League unless they could win their last game of the season against Plymouth Argyle.

If your team ever finds itself needing a last-gasp win, here's how to do it the Carlisle way –

THE GOAL-SCORING GOALKEEPER WHO WOULDN'T HAVE SCORED IF HE'D BEEN A BETTER GOALKEEPER AWARD...

Jimmy Glass, the goalkeeper who scored the vital last-minute goal for Carlisle United – and he wasn't even a Carlisle player. He was only on loan from Swindon, because he hadn't been able to get into their team!

HE DOESN'T DO THAT FOR US!

THE BOOK MOST LIKELY TO REVEAL WHO MIGHT TURN OUT TO BE A GOAL-SCORING GOALKEEPER AWARD...

The Professional Footballer's Association Fact-File, published every year. The 1998–99 edition said of Jimmy Glass: "He's not afraid to come off his line"!

I DON'T MIND YOU COMING OFF YOUR LINE, JIM, I'M JUST NOT TOO SURE ABOUT YOU GOING SHOPPING

SCOTTISH LEAGUE

Scottish footballers have always been prominent in the English Football League. Liverpool had a team of ten Scottish outfield players in 1893 and, in the old Third Division (North) in 1955 Accrington Stanley became the first League team to field an entire side of Scots.

Are you non-Scottish and surprised? You shouldn't be. If there's one League that is almost as legendary as the Football League it's the Scottish League...

The tartan timeline

1867 Queens Park, Scotland's oldest League club, is formed. They play in the English FA Cup, losing in the final twice! They stop when the Scottish FA Cup begins in 1874 – and win that trophy three years running.

1890 The Scottish League is formed. The newspaper *Scottish Sport* isn't impressed. It says the idea is all about "money-making and money-grabbing." It's right, too. Just like William McGregor's Football League, the Scots clubs need the money from regular games to pay players.

1893 A Second Division is added.

1923 A Third Division is added.

1926 The Third Division is removed!

1945 Numbered divisions disappear altogether!

When the Scottish League begins again after World War Two it has three divisions, called A, B and C.

1946 The Scots invent a new competition – the Scottish League Cup – to be played for only by clubs in the Scottish League. The slow Football League won't invent the same sort of competition for another 14 years.

1950 Now the C division disappears! Is it because Scots clubs prefer to travel straight from A to B?

1956 Maybe not. The A and B divisions go back to being called the First and Second Divisions.

1970 Whichever way it's going, the Scottish League leads the Football League by six years when it replaces goal average with goal difference as a way of dividing teams with the same number of points.

1975 It's back to a three-division league, this time with a Premier Division of ten teams and First and Second Divisions of 14 teams each. It's a reorganization which puts the Scottish League ahead of the world. No other league has a smaller division just for the best few teams and the FA Premiership won't exist for another 17 years.

1984 The Scottish League Cup is sponsored by the Danish lager company, Skol. Only one problem – because of a ban on taking drinks into football matches, fans can't buy Skol lager at Skol Cup matches!

1994 The League expands to four divisions of ten teams, with a Premier League and Divisions One, Two and Three. It's the biggest league the Scots have had. How long will it last?

1998 Not long. Just like the top English clubs did in 1992, the Scottish Premier League teams form a new league called … the Scottish Premier League! What's changed? Only that it's run by the Scottish Football Association rather than the Scottish League. Even fewer fans notice the change than did in England!

Scottish League legends

Well, they're not legends exactly. They're facts. They're just a bit incredible, that's all...

League losses

The first-ever Scottish League season began with 11 of these 12 teams. Which is the odd one out?

Abercorn
The Borderers
Cambuslang
Celtic
Cowlairs
Dumbarton
Heart of Midlothian
Rangers
Renton
St Mirren
Third Lanark
Vale of Leven

Answer: The Borderers. This is the nickname of the current Scottish League team Berwick Rangers – who began life in the Northumberland League because the town is actually just on the English side of the border! They're the only English team in the Scottish League.

LOOK, EITHER YOU'RE IN THIS LEAGUE OR YOU'RE NOT!

Berwick may have been the odd team out because they didn't start the first-ever Scottish League season – but there's another odd team out in the list as well. A team that started the first League season, but didn't actually finish it...

Runaway Renton

During their short stay in the big-time (they finally left the Scottish League in 1898), Renton made their mark in quite a few ways.

Some were good...

- In 1886–87 they entered the English FA Cup. This was held by Blackburn Rovers, who'd won it three years in a row ... and Renton knocked them out!
- In 1890 they scored the first Scottish League goal, in the first minute of their match against Celtic.

And some were bad...

- In 1894–5 they became the first team not to turn up for a League match, a Second Division game against Dundee Wanderers (who became the first team to be awarded League points without having to play a game)!

But the worst of the lot happened in 1890, when Renton were disqualified from the Scottish League in mid-season. This was officially because they'd broken League rules and played a game against a suspended team, Edinburgh Saints. But at the time, the Scottish League organizers were also looking suspiciously at Renton themselves.

Question: What had they discovered that looked decidedly dodgy?

a) Renton had spent a large amount of money on chickens.

b) The grass on Renton's pitch looked the same as some stolen from a local park.

ABOUT THIS NEW PITCH OF YOURS...

c) Renton's players all had their own motor cars.

Answer: a) They suspected that the money was actually being paid illegally to the Renton players – even though Renton claimed they really had

bought chickens to make the "chicken bree" (soup)
the players trained on!

The team that went backwards

Port Glasgow Athletic played in the Scottish League
Division Two. In the 1893–94 season they'd managed
to pick up six points from two wins and two draws.
Unfortunately, though, in some of their games they'd
fielded a player they hadn't signed properly. In
stepped the Scottish League officials.

One of those games had been a win for Port Glasgow
against a team called Northern – so they had two
points deducted, bringing them down to four.

Another of the games was a drawn match against
Clyde – so that one point was lost as well. Now they
were down to three points.

Finally, the Scottish League decided that Port
Glasgow should be punished for what they'd done.
What would be a suitable punishment? wondered
the League Committee. Then somebody came up
with a suggestion. A fine! Money? No, four points!

So Port Glasgow Athletic had another four points
taken away from the three they'd got ... leaving them
with minus one and the record (until they managed

to draw their next game) of being the only scatty Scottish League team to have fewer points during a season than the zero points they started with!

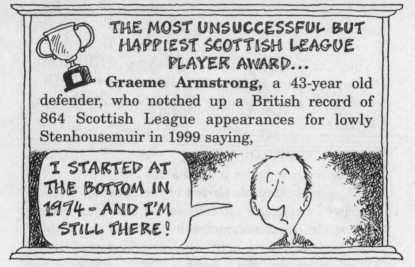

THE MOST UNSUCCESSFUL BUT HAPPIEST SCOTTISH LEAGUE PLAYER AWARD...

Graeme Armstrong, a 43-year old defender, who notched up a British record of 864 Scottish League appearances for lowly Stenhousemuir in 1999 saying,

I STARTED AT THE BOTTOM IN 1974 - AND I'M STILL THERE!

The Old Firm: Celtic and Rangers

Two clubs have dominated the Scottish League: Glasgow Celtic and Glasgow Rangers, otherwise known as "The Old Firm". Their rivalry dates back to the very beginnings of the game in Scotland.

Try to sort out who came out on top at various times with this Old Firm facts quiz. The answer to each question is either *Celtic* or *Rangers*.

1 They were the first of the rivals to win the Scottish League, getting their hands on the trophy the first time it was awarded in 1890–91.

2 They raced away with the title in 1898–99 by becoming the first and only British team to win every one of their (18) League games.

86

3 Celtic and Rangers finished the 1904–05 season level on points. Rangers' goal record was 83 scored, 28 conceded; Celtic's was 68 scored and 31 conceded. Which of them was awarded the championship trophy?

4 They achieved the first-ever League and Scottish FA Cup "double" in 1906–07, winning the League by seven points and beating Hearts 3-0 in the Cup Final.

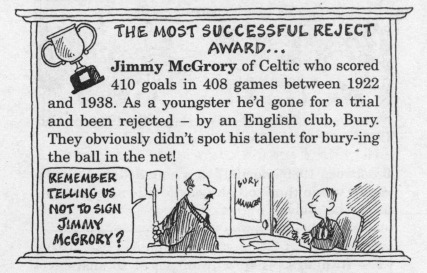

THE MOST SUCCESSFUL REJECT AWARD...

Jimmy McGrory of Celtic who scored 410 goals in 408 games between 1922 and 1938. As a youngster he'd gone for a trial and been rejected – by an English club, Bury. They obviously didn't spot his talent for bury-ing the ball in the net!

REMEMBER TELLING US NOT TO SIGN JIMMY McGRORY?

BURY MANAGER

5 Rangers beat Celtic 2-1 on 2 January, 1939, in what's become an annual New Years' Holiday league match. The result isn't a record this time, it's the size of the crowd that's astonishing as 118,567 pack in to watch – the only time a crowd of over 100,000 has been known for a League match in Britain.

At which of the two teams' grounds was the game played?

6 Which of the rivals notched up another record in 1957 as they walloped the other 7-1 in the Scottish League Cup Final?

7 They were totally untouchable in 1967. They won every competition they entered, including becoming the first British club to win the European Champions Cup.

8 Between 1966 and 1974 they win the Scottish League a record nine seasons in a row!

9 Between 1989 and 1997 they equalled their rival's record to win the Scottish League title nine times in a row themselves.

Answers:
1 – Rangers. They only managed to share it, though. That first League Championship was shared with Dumbarton as the two sides finished on the same number of points.
2 – Rangers.
3 – Celtic. If they'd been playing in the Football League, Rangers would have been clear champions on goal average. But the Scottish League were playing to different rules. Theirs

said that if the top teams were level on points they had to have a play-off match. They did – and Celtic won it to become champions!

4 – Celtic.

5 – Rangers' ground, Ibrox Park. You could say they did well to Celtic-kets!!

6 – Celtic. And the record? 7-1 is the highest score recorded in any British Cup Final.

7 – Celtic.

8 – Celtic.

9 – Rangers.

THE MOST SUCCESSFUL HOME-GROWN TEAM AWARD...

Celtic, in 1966–67. Nowadays, no champion team is without its collection of stars from other countries. Celtic's team wasn't just all-Scottish – it was just about all-Glaswegian. Every single player had been born no more than 30 miles from the city.

Terrible troubles

Old Firm matches may have produced lots of fabulous football but, sadly, they've seen some terrible troubles as well.

The furious final

In 1908–9 Celtic and Rangers met each other in the Scottish FA Cup Final and drew 2-2. They tried again in a replay, but this time the score was 1-1 at the end of 90 minutes. The players and crowd were expecting extra time to be played, but the rules of the competition said that it was the end of the game and that there had to be another replay.

So the players left the field ... only for the seething spectators to run on and start shouting for them to come out again. And when the police raced on to try and clear the pitch, the furious fans turned really fiery. How fiery? By trying to set bits of the stadium alight, that's how fiery! What did they use as fuel?

Answer: a) Fortunately the fires didn't get out of hand. Afterwards, it was the turn of the Scottish FA to turn fiery. To teach the fans a lesson they decided not to award the Scottish FA Cup to either club that season, the only time this has ever happened.

The deadly dive

Saturday 5 September, 1931. Rangers were on the attack. The ball ran loose into the Celtic penalty area. Rangers' forward Sam English raced after it. From the opposite direction darted Celtic's goalkeeper, John Thompson...

It was the sort of incident that happened regularly in football matches everywhere. But on this occasion the results were to be tragic. As he dived at English's feet, the Celtic goalkeeper was cracked on the head by the forward's knee. He collapsed and was carried off to hospital. He died that evening.

More than 30,000 attended John Thompson's funeral and Celtic fans still visit his grave.

Too many of them cared nothing for how poor Sam English felt, though, even though the collision had been a complete accident. Just a year later he'd left Scotland to play in England, forced out by the terrible booing and comments he'd had to suffer whenever he played.

The Ibrox tragedy
Forty years on, in 1971, came an even worse tragedy. This time it was the fans who suffered. It happened on 2 January, at Rangers' ground, Ibrox Stadium.

With two minutes to go in the match, Celtic were ahead 1-0. Hundreds of disappointed Rangers fans began pouring out of the ground and down the high stone stairways. Suddenly, a huge roar went up. Rangers had equalized!

On one of the stairways, dozens of fans turned back and tried to race up to get into the ground again. But all they did was run into the fans coming the opposite way and cause a terrible crush. Some of the fans tripped and fell. They panicked. Others fell on top of them, but now the game had ended and the rest of the 80,000 crowd was trying to leave Ibrox...

Sixty-six fans died.

Guilty, Your Honour #1

With crowd trouble taking place (and still taking place, unfortunately) at so many Celtic v Rangers games, it doesn't help if the players themselves start having a punch-up.

That's what the police thought in October 1987, anyway. After a fight during the match, Rangers defender Terry Butcher and goalkeeper Chris Woods were both taken to court and found guilty of "disorderly conduct on the field of play". They were relieved only to be fined – they could both have been thrown into jail!

Guilty, Your Honour #2

Finally, the case of a crooked fan who escaped. In May 1998, a dozy magistrate at Glasgow's District Court had to decide on an appropriate sentence for the man in the dock before him. Should he go to prison, or not?

He looked at the crook, saw he was wearing a Rangers shirt ... and let him walk away a free man! Before he left the magistrate said, "I see you're a Rangers supporter," then added – what?

a) "Up the "Gers!"
b) "You've suffered enough!"
c) "I hate Celtic too!"

Answer: b). An odd comment, seeing as how Rangers had won the League for the previous nine years!

THE MOST SHORT-SIGHTED MAGISTRATE AWARD...

The magistrate at Glasgow District Court. The fan wasn't wearing a Rangers replica shirt at all. He was wearing a Newcastle United away strip!

IS THIS THE FIRST TIME YOU'VE BEEN UP BEFORE ME, MISS?

THE LEAGUE CUP

Until 1960, English football only had two club competitions:

- The FA Cup, run by the Football Association
- The League, run by the Football League

What was (and still is) the difference between the Football Association and the Football League? Simple...

- The Football League organization can only boss around teams in the League.
- The Football Association can boss every team around, right from the top league teams down to the lowest school teams, like yours! That's because they're the people who make the rules for football, and the biggest rule of the lot is that a team can't play in competition unless it's joined to the FA.

Then, in 1960, the League organizers had a big idea...

And so, in the 1960–61 season, the Football League Cup began. This competition could only be entered by teams in the League and not, unlike the FA Cup,[1] by little non-league teams (who might cause red faces by winning their cup-ties).

Unfortunately, not all the League clubs thought the new competition was a good idea. Arsenal, Sheffield Wednesday, Tottenham, West Bromwich Albion and Wolves (the big clubs of the day) all refused to take part, saying they were playing too many games already.

1 See *Foul Football: The Phenomenal FA Cup* for the rules and much more besides!

In the end, old First Division club Aston Villa beat old Second Division Rotherham United to become the first League Cup winners.

Question: What was odd about that 1960–61 League Cup final?
a) It was played over two legs.
b) It was decided by a penalty shoot-out.
c) It took place the following season.

> **Answer: c) ... and a).** That first final was held over until the start of the 1961–62 season. Rotherham won the first leg 2-0, but Aston Villa won the second leg 3-0 to take the cup.

The competition still wasn't popular, though. The following season even fewer clubs took part and even when more did join in they didn't take it very seriously ... until the 1966–67 season.

Question: What happened to change the big clubs' minds?
a) The two-legged final was scrapped and replaced by a one-game final at Wembley Stadium.
b) The winners were awarded a place in a European competition, The Fairs Cup (later the UEFA Cup), provided they were a First Division side.

> **Answer: a) AND b) ... but mostly b).** While a big final day out at Wembley was attractive, it was the chance of qualifying for Europe that was the thing the big clubs liked most. In other words, the clubs who'd said they were playing too many

games now agreed to play some more games because it gave them a chance of qualifying for a competition that would mean they played even more games on top of those they hadn't wanted to play in the first place! Get it?!!

Rip-roaring Rangers

That first Wembley League Cup Final was a magical day for little Queens Park Rangers of the old Third Division. They were up against the League Cup holders, West Bromwich Albion, and weren't given much of a chance. By half-time, that's the way it looked. Rangers were 0-2 down.

urged their manager, Alec Stock, at half-time.

So they did...

After 63 minutes, Rangers made it 1-2. West Bromwich weren't worried. Then this happened. Try it in your next school match if you're losing...

Get the ball on the half-way line

Start dribbling forward, even though (like unworried West Brom) the other team have got five players between you and the goal...

Mesmerize one defender and tie another couple in knots with your dribbling skills...

Keep going until you reach the edge of the penalty area...

Let fly with a shot...

Then watch it ping off a post and into the net for an equalizer!

PING!

That's what Rangers' star forward Rodney Marsh did in the 75th minute to make the score 2-2. West Bromwich were worried now!

But rip-roaring Rangers were running riot. With nine minutes to go they scored again to make it 3-2. They'd become the first side from the old Third Division ever to win a major knock-out trophy.

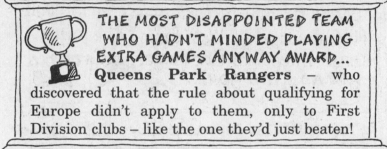

THE MOST DISAPPOINTED TEAM WHO HADN'T MINDED PLAYING EXTRA GAMES ANYWAY AWARD... **Queens Park Rangers** – who discovered that the rule about qualifying for Europe didn't apply to them, only to First Division clubs – like the one they'd just beaten!

Four funny League Cup facts

1 It must hold the record for the competition with the funniest name. After 20 years as a plain old League Cup, it has since been named after whichever company are paying big money to have their product linked with it. The latest score is Drinks 3, Big Stores 2. Littlewoods (1987–90) and Rumbelows (1991–92, until they went bust!) were the stores ... but which are the three League Cup drinks out of these five?

BEER   COLA   COFFEE   MILK   TEA

Answer: Milk (It was known as The Milk Cup from 1982–86), **Coca-Cola** (1993–98) and **Beer** (The Worthington Cup, from 1999). It hasn't yet been called either The Coffee Cup or The Tea Cup, but it's probably only a matter of time.

2 The Littlewoods Cup was actually one of the oldest football trophies in the world, dating back to 1895. It had originally been awarded to the winners of a tournament run by ship-building firms in the North-East of England – then locked in a cupboard and forgotten about!

3 The record League Cup score is 9-1, recorded in September 1964 by Workington against Barrow. It's a score that's unlikely to be equalled in the competition – not by those two teams anyway, because they've both been kicked out of the League since then! Barrow were replaced by Hereford in 1972 and Workington by Wimbledon in 1977.

4 Nottingham Forest had a great run in the competition between 1978–80, reaching the final three years in a row. They won the first two, but lost the third. In 1977–78 their England international goalkeeper, Peter Shilton, couldn't play because he'd already appeared in the competition that season for his previous club. So Chris Woods, Forest's 18-year-old reserve goalkeeper, took Shilton's place in every round right up to the final – where he picked up a League Cup winner's medal before he'd played his first League game!

LEGENDARY WORLD LEAGUES

Nowadays there are league competitions all over the world. You probably play in one yourself. But is it as small as the one held in the Scilly Islands? In 1959, they had the smallest league in the British Isles – with how many teams?

a) Two.

b) Four.

c) Six.

Answer: a) – St Mary's Rovers and St Mary's Rangers. It had been a four-team league until the other two teams, St Martin and Tresco played each other. After their game ended with a St Martin's player nursing a broken leg and a Tresco player suffering a broken neck, both sides withdrew from League football!

D'YOU THINK YOU'LL BE FIT ENOUGH TO PLAY SATURDAY?

How long has your league been going? It won't have started as long ago as 1888, like the Football League, but it might be older than the leagues in some countries.

Now's your chance to find out. Here are 15 countries.

Sort their league competitions into three age divisions, like this –

First Division: if you think their league started before 1900.

Second Division: if you think their league started between 1901 and 1930.

Third Division: if you think their league started after 1930.

Answers:

First Division: Argentina (They had an amateur league by 1891, although a league for professional teams didn't start until 1931); Northern Ireland (also 1891); Belgium (1896); Holland (1898); India (Yes, in 1898! it was started by British soldiers and the first champions were The Gloucestershire Regiment!).

Second Division: Brazil (1902 – although only in one of their biggest cities, Sao Paulo. The Brazilian national championship didn't start until 1967. Why? Because, at 64 times the size of England, the country is so gigantic that before air travel, playing an away game would have meant leaving home for ages!)

Germany (1903; a collection of regional leagues, with the winners going into play-off matches to decide the overall champions); Mexico (also 1903); Austria (1912); Italy (1921 – like Germany's, a regional competition. We're not counting the Italian league of 1898, because it only had four teams and was all over and done with in a single day!); Spain (1929).

Third Division: France (1933); Egypt (1949); Japan (1965); USA (1967).

Global goofs and world woes

With all these league competitions around the world, there are bound to be differences between them. But some things are always the same –

especially the way every league manages to produce funny stories.

Let's chase a league title round the world and have a look at some...

It's true!

In 2000, after cases of players taking bribes to fix the results of matches in their S-league, the Singapore Football Association decided to try and stop it ever happening again by – what?

a) Checking players' bank accounts every Monday morning.

b) Making players take lie-detector tests.

c) Paying players more money than the bribe if they owned up.

Answer: b) And presumably asking them questions like: "Did you take money to lose that game 10-0, or are you simply useless?"

Bundesliga bungles

Germany's national League, *The Bundesliga*, began in 1962. Until then, the German champions had been decided by play-offs between the winners of the different regional leagues around the country.

Young as it is, though, the *Bundesliga* has had its share of problems and nutty happenings. See if you can sort out the truth in this quartet!

1 Before the final games of the 1977–78 season, FC Cologne and Borussia Monchengladbach were level on points, with Cologne having a far better goal difference. If "Gladbach" were going to overtake them they'd have to score ten more goals.

What was most suspicious was that they almost did! If Cologne hadn't won their own game 5-0, they'd have been in trouble – because Gladbach beat close neighbours Borussia Dortmund 12-0!

Question: Was it a fix? Yes or No.

Answer: No. The Dortmund goalkeeper had heard the day before the game that the club were going to buy somebody to replace him. When the game took place he was thinking more about this bad news than he was about stopping shots!

2 Another team, Bayern Munich, had trouble with its players in 1998. Concerned that they were losing too many league points because some of their men were staying out too late at night, the club told them they had to be in bed early.

Question: What did they do to make sure the rule was followed?

a) Put "big brother" cameras in their bedrooms.

b) Have them followed by private detectives.

c) Give them alarm clocks with the club badge on.

Answer: b) The detectives had to report back if the players weren't in bed by 11.30 p.m. In other words, the players could have a ball just so long as it wasn't one of Cinderella's midnight sort!

3 In December 1999, *Bundesliga* club Hertha Berlin had a cracker of an idea for getting their fans to come to their league match against Kaiserslauten instead of going Christmas shopping: they'd let them in free if they turned up wearing a – what?

a) Father Christmas outfit.

b) Set of reindeer's horns.

c) Sprig of holly in their hair.

Answer: a) It worked; there were 500 white-bearded, red-suited supporters around the ground.

4 In 1999, FC Nurnberg sent in an official complaint to the German FA after they'd been beaten 3-0 by Dortmund. What were they protesting about?
a) The crowd had been too noisy.
b) The football had been out of shape.
c) The referee had been a woman.

Answer: a) Before the game 40,000 toy trumpets had been given out to the spectators. Nurnberg claimed their players hadn't been able to concentrate on the game because of all the terrible trumpeting that started up whenever they tried to attack!

Japanese jottings
The professional Japanese J-League began in 1993. Many overseas players arrived to join native Japanese footballers who were hoping to improve by mixing with experienced stars. They had a lot to learn. One overseas player, Bulgarian international Hristo Stoichkov, said:

THE JAPANESE ARE FAR TOO NICE. ONCE, A PLAYER FOULED ME THEN FOLLOWED ME ROUND THE FIELD FOR A GOOD FIVE MINUTES APOLOGIZING! FOOTBALL IS A GAME FOR MEN!

SORRY!

Eddie Thomson, Australian manager of J-league team Sanfrecce Hiroshima, had a good idea what they had to do to improve. In 1999, he said:

THEY NEED TO GET BACK TO PLAYING AND STOP WORRYING ABOUT THEIR HAIRCUTS!

You cannot be serie-as!!

Players get pretty excitable in Serie A, the top Italian league, too – but not many get sent off without even touching the ball! That's what the Lazio subsitute, Ammoniaci, managed to achieve during their big local derby against Roma in 1979.

Ammoniaci had been yelling nasty things at the Roma players all through the game – especially at Roma's midfield player, Boni. Finally, Ammoniaci got the chance to do something more than shout. In the 89th minute a Lazio player was substituted and on he raced – straight towards Boni! What did Ammoniaci do?

a) Kick Boni up the bum.

b) Pretend Boni had kicked him.

Answer: b) The Lazio substitute hurled himself at Boni, then collapsed writhing on the ground. Moments later Ammoniaci was back on his feet and heading for the dressing room. The referee had sent him off for pretending he'd been fouled!

With excitable players like that, maybe it was natural that if any country was going to experiment with having two referees controlling a match instead of just one poor individual, then it was going to be Italy.

It happened in 1999, during a match between Sampdoria and Bologna. Did it work well? Nobody had a chance to find out, mainly because the biggest decision the referees had to make wasn't concerned with the players' behaviour at all. When the

Sampdoria fans refused to stop throwing missiles at the Bologna and ex-Sampdoria goalkeeper Gianluca Pagliuca, the referees put their heads together – and abandoned the game!

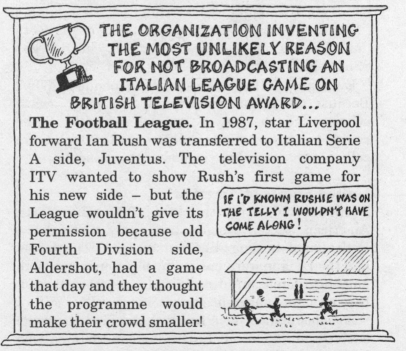

THE ORGANIZATION INVENTING THE MOST UNLIKELY REASON FOR NOT BROADCASTING AN ITALIAN LEAGUE GAME ON BRITISH TELEVISION AWARD...

The Football League. In 1987, star Liverpool forward Ian Rush was transferred to Italian Serie A side, Juventus. The television company ITV wanted to show Rush's first game for his new side – but the League wouldn't give its permission because old Fourth Division side, Aldershot, had a game that day and they thought the programme would make their crowd smaller!

IF I'D KNOWN RUSHIE WAS ON THE TELLY I WOULDN'T HAVE COME ALONG!

They take discipline seriously in Italy. How seriously? So seriously that in 1995 a player was suspended – even though he was dead! Just a week after

Luigi Collucio was sent off during a match in one of the regional leagues, he was shot dead in a battle with some members of a different kind of team: the Mafia.

HE'S NOT THE PLAYER HE WAS

Even so, Collucio was still suspended. Why? Because the league operated a "fair play" award scheme and the player's punishment had to be counted in case it made a difference to which team collected the award at the end of the season!

United Stunts of America

Between 1967 and the late 1980s the North American Soccer League tried hard to make a professional League work in the USA. The teams and the League were backed by big-money sponsors and they didn't only bring in players from abroad, they brought in league organizers as well.

Somebody must have heard that a big idea needs a Scotsman in charge, because one of the men who came in was Sir George Graham, who used to be the secretary of the Scottish FA. He was full of enthusiasm, saying:

WHEN ENGLAND GAVE
SOCCER TO THE WORLD
THE UNITED STATES WAS
SOMEHOW MISSED OUT.
NOW, A HUNDRED YEARS
ON, THAT GAP CAN BE
FILLED WITH A WORLD-
BEATING DEMONSTRATION
OF HOW IT SHOULD BE DONE!

But the league had a hard job selling the game to the public. Football in America meant American football – a game played with an oval ball that's rarely kicked! Soccer was a whole different ball game...

Another of the league's organizers, ex-Welsh international Phil Woosnam, tried to explain the basics of the game:

THE RULES ARE VERY
SIMPLE. BASICALLY, IF
IT MOVES KICK IT... AND
IF IT DOESN'T MOVE, KICK
IT UNTIL IT DOES!

THE AMERICAN LEAGUE TEAM
WITH THE MOST CONFUSED
SUPPORTERS AWARD...
Baltimore Bays. During their opening league match against Atlanta Chiefs, Baltimore lost no fewer than 12 footballs

because the crowd repeatedly followed the custom amongst American baseball fans — of keeping any ball they managed to catch!

Filled with players from overseas, the American League eventually got under way. Just like the Football League, the American League changed the rules as it went along but the pattern was always the same. Teams played each other in small leagues, with the top teams meeting later in play-off matches to decide the overall champions.

You could tell where any team was based from its name. Team names usually had two parts and the first part always told you which big American or Canadian city the team came from. How about the second part? Some would say that it was a word telling you how the team played! Here are some of them. Try to pair up the two halves of the names!

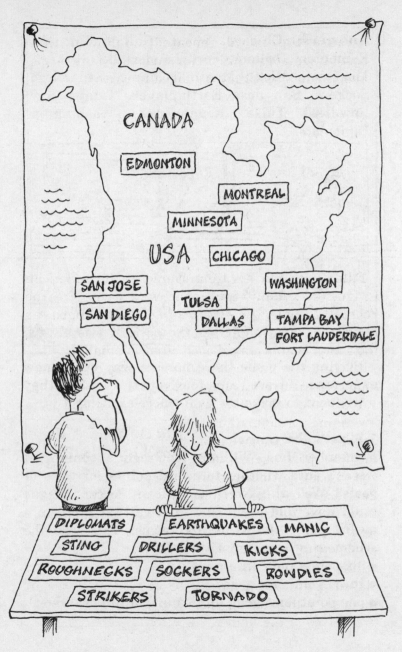

Answers: Chicago Sting, Dallas Tornado, Edmonton Drillers, Fort Lauderdale Strikers, Minnesota Kicks, Montreal Manic, San Diego Sockers, San Jose Earthquakes, Tampa Bay Rowdies, Tulsa Roughnecks, Washington Diplomats.

Playing the game the American way was a new experience. Here are four of the rules they introduced to make the game more exciting:

1 What's the point?
Remember how William McGregor's committee weren't sure whether to award points for wins or goals? Well the North American Soccer League could have told them how to solve that problem – award points for wins *and* goals. This was the scheme they came up with at first:
- six points for a win
- three points for a tie
- one point for a goal, up to a maximum of three.

116

Question: Wonderful Wildcats beat Shocking Shooters 6-2; how many points do each team earn?

Answer: Wonderful Wildcats get nine points (six for the win, three for their first 3 goals); Shocking Shooters get two points (for their goals).

Later this scheme was changed to nine points for a win, one point for a first goal, two for a second and three for a third (giving Wonderful Wildcats 15 points and Shocking Shooters 3 points)

2 Aagh! Sudden death!

Drawn – called tied – matches weren't put up with for long. Spectators wanted to see one team or the other become the match winner.

So, if the scores were level at the end of full-time, the teams went into a period of sudden-death over-time. The first team to score a goal in this period were the winners, and the game stopped at once!

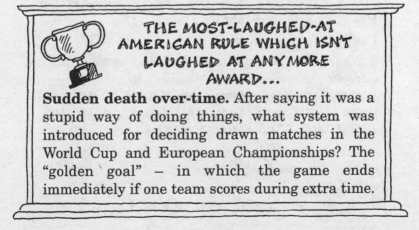

THE MOST-LAUGHED-AT AMERICAN RULE WHICH ISN'T LAUGHED AT ANYMORE AWARD...

Sudden death over-time. After saying it was a stupid way of doing things, what system was introduced for deciding drawn matches in the World Cup and European Championships? The "golden goal" – in which the game ends immediately if one team scores during extra time.

3 Paying the penalty!

If the match was still tied after the sudden-death period, it was time for a penalty shoot-out ... American-style. Here's how to do it the next time your team draws a match.

PICK FIVE PLAYERS FROM EACH SIDE TO TAKE THE PENALTIES, BUT TELL THEM NOT TO PUT THE BALL ON THE PENALTY SPOT...

INSTEAD, PLAYERS HAVE TO TAKE THE BALL 35 YARDS (ABOUT 30 METRES) AWAY FROM GOAL...

THEN, WHEN THE WHISTLE BLOWS, THE PLAYER DRIBBLES IT FORWARD...

OPPOSING GOALKEEPERS DON'T HAVE TO STAY ON THEIR LINE, EITHER; THEY CAN COME CHARGING OUT TO MEET THE PENALTY TAKER...

IF YOU'RE TAKING THE PENALTY IT'S UP TO YOU WHAT YOU DO NEXT. YOU CAN BLAST A SHOT, DRIBBLE THE BALL AROUND THE KEEPER AND TAP IT INTO THE NET, FLICK IT ON TO YOUR NOSE AND RUN ALL THE WAY - WHATEVER YOU LIKE...

JUST SO LONG AS YOU DO IT INSIDE FIVE SECONDS. TAKE ANY LONGER THAN THAT (AND YOU WILL IF THE KEEPER GRABS THE BALL) AND YOU'VE MISSED!

TICK! TICK! TICK!

4 Cheers!

Finally, football for TV viewers was a bit different as well.

There's some exciting stuff being played. Your team are surging onto the attack. Your star striker is racing towards goal. Past one defender he goes, then another.

He's reached the edge of the penalty area. It's the perfect shooting chance! He draws back his foot. He's going to hit a thunderbolt! You're on the edge of your seat. It's the moment you've been waiting for all game! Will he score? Will you see your team go ahead?

119

Not if it's time for an advertisement, you won't! The first televised league game between Baltimore Bays and Atlanta Chiefs was interrupted by ten beer adverts, each lasting for a minute!

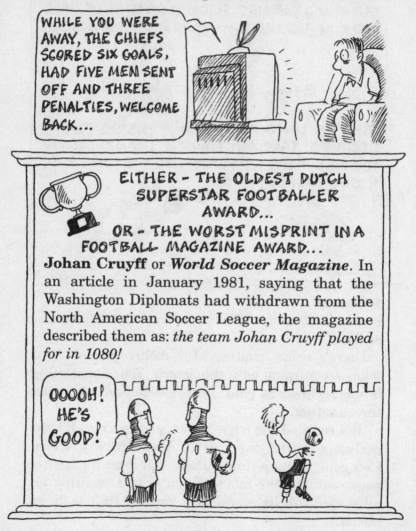

WHILE YOU WERE AWAY, THE CHIEFS SCORED SIX GOALS, HAD FIVE MEN SENT OFF AND THREE PENALTIES, WELCOME BACK...

EITHER - THE OLDEST DUTCH SUPERSTAR FOOTBALLER AWARD...
OR - THE WORST MISPRINT IN A FOOTBALL MAGAZINE AWARD...

Johan Cruyff or *World Soccer Magazine*. In an article in January 1981, saying that the Washington Diplomats had withdrawn from the North American Soccer League, the magazine described them as: *the team Johan Cruyff played for in 1080!*

OOOOH! HE'S GOOD!

THE LEGENDARY FIRSTS QUIZ

The Football League is legendary because William McGregor's big idea produced the first competition of its kind. So it seems a good idea – a big idea, even! – to end this book with a quiz about ten legendary league firsts.

You get two points for every right answer. Let's see if you're on championship form!

1 In 1891–92, Sunderland and Aston Villa were the first league teams to – what?
a) Not win a game all season.
b) Not draw a game all season.
c) Not lose a game all season.

2 On 5 December, 1931 in the old First Division, Newcastle United and Portsmouth were the first (and, so far, only) teams to play a whole League game without either of them winning a – what?
a) Penalty.
b) Free-kick.
c) Corner.

3 Kenny Dalglish, of Celtic and then Liverpool, was the first player to do what in both the English and Scottish Leagues?
a) Win league championship medals.
b) Score 100 league goals.
c) Become manager of his old team.

4 On 20 September, 1890, Sunderland beat West Bromwich Albion 4-0 ... but didn't increase their points total because they'd become the first League team to break a League rule and – what?

a) Be told to replay their game.

b) Be expelled from the League.

c) Be fined League points.

5 In the 1903–04 season, after playing just 450 Football League games, Aston Villa became the first team to have scored how many League goals?

a) 500

b) 750

c) 1000

6 The League match played at Highbury on 22 January, 1927, between Arsenal and Sheffield United, was the first to – what?

a) Have highlights shown on the TV news.

b) Be broadcast live on radio.

c) Feature in a newspaper spot-the-ball competition.

7 On 13 April, 1936, the number ten proved to be lucky for Luton Town's centre-forward Joe Payne as he became the only League player to – what?

a) Score ten goals in a match.

b) Wear the number ten on his shirt.

c) Be sent off after ten minutes.

8 The game in which Millwall beat Fulham 1-0 in the old Second Division on 20 January, 1974 was a famous first – but it had nothing to do with the result or the two teams. It was a first because of the day. Why?

a) It was the first League game played on a Sunday.

b) It the was the first mid-week League game.

c) It was the first League match played in the morning.

THIS IS PLAYING HAVOC WITH MY CORNFLAKES

9 In the 1957–58 season, Manchester City became the first (and, so far, only) League team to do – what?

a) Win and give away 30 penalties.

b) Win, draw and lose the same number of games.

c) Score and give away 100 goals.

10 The first foreign player turned out for a Football League team in what season?

a) 1908–09

b) 1928–29

c) 1948–49

Answers:

1b) Aston Villa came fourth, winning 15 games and losing 11; as for Sunderland, they lost five and won 21 to finish as League Champions!

2c) Surprise, surprise, the game ended in a 0-0 draw.

3b) And he ended up doing **a)** and **c)** as well.

4c) They were fined two points for playing the new signing, Scots international goalkeeper Ned Doig, before his transfer had been approved.

5c) Something for William McGregor to boast about!

6b) Listeners were given a diagram for the pitch divided into eight squares and while one commentator described what was going on, another said what square the ball was in. Ever heard of the saying "back to square one", meaning to start again? That's where it came from!

7a) Luton beat Bristol Rovers 12-0 in the old Third Division (South) and Joe proved to be a right Payne by scoring ten of them. It was his first game at centre-forward because Luton's two regulars were both injured!

8a)

9c) They scored 104 and let in 100 to finish fifth in the old First Division.

10a) He was a German named Max Seeburg whose first League game was for Tottenham Hotspur.

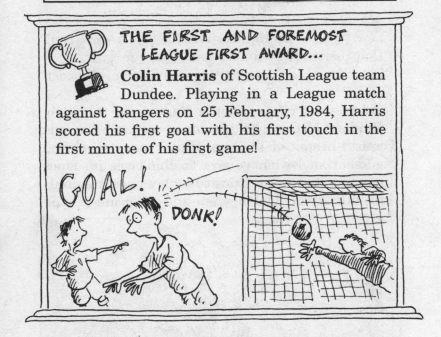

THE FIRST AND FOREMOST LEAGUE FIRST AWARD...

Colin Harris of Scottish League team Dundee. Playing in a League match against Rangers on 25 February, 1984, Harris scored his first goal with his first touch in the first minute of his first game!

GOAL!

DONK!

So, how did you get on? There were a maximum of 20 points to be picked up in that quiz.

18–20 points: Champion!

10–16 points: Mid-table position

0–8 points: Doomed to relegation!

* * *

AND FINALLY...

Do you dream of becoming a Premier League footballer one day? Plenty of boys – and girls – do, but very few manage it. Even so, that needn't be the end of your dreams.

William McGregor's big idea was only for one Football League of 12 teams. But it was such a good big idea that, as you've seen in this book, it's since spread far and wide. Nowadays there are hundreds and hundreds of leagues, and thousands and thousands of teams.

What's more, if you live in England, all these leagues are joined together in what's called the "league pyramid". That means that even if you're only playing for Not-Very-Good United in the Not-Very-Good League you've still got plenty to go for.

One good season, and your team could be promoted to the next league up. Another good season, and you could move up again...

String enough good seasons together and you could make it to the Conference League. Another one, and you'd be in Third Division ... the Second ... the First ... and finally the Premiership!

A dream? Of course it is. But what was William McGregor's big idea if it wasn't a dream as well? So keep playing – and who knows, you could find yourself adding to the legend of the most legendary of all legendary leagues!